ANIMAL ENCOUNTER
BUCKET LIST

BY EMMA HUDDLESTON

CONTENT CONSULTANT
Christopher S. DePerno, PhD
Professor, Fisheries, Wildlife, and Conservation Biology
North Carolina State University

Cover image: Some animal encounters, such as those at zoos, allow
visitors to see animals up close.

Core Library

An Imprint of Abdo Publishing
abdobooks.com

abdobooks.com

Published by Abdo Publishing, a division of ABDO, PO Box 398166, Minneapolis, Minnesota 55439. Copyright © 2022 by Abdo Consulting Group, Inc. International copyrights reserved in all countries. No part of this book may be reproduced in any form without written permission from the publisher. Core Library™ is a trademark and logo of Abdo Publishing.

Printed in the United States of America, North Mankato, Minnesota.
102021
012022

Cover Photo: Andrey Gudkov/Shutterstock Images
Interior Photos: BlueOrange Studio/Shutterstock Images, 4–5; Guenter Guni/iStockphoto, 7; Cheryl Ramalho/iStockphoto, 8; iStockphoto, 10; Karen Crewe/Shutterstock Images, 12–13; Shutterstock Images, 16, 18, 19 (bottom left), 19 (bottom right); Elena Schweitzer/Shutterstock Images, 19 (top left); J. Ray Upchurch/iStockphoto, 19 (top right); Terri Lea Mays/iStockphoto, 22–23; Andy Astbury/iStockphoto, 27; Rodney Cammauf/National Park Service, 28; Red Line Editorial, 30, 42–43; Mongkolchon Akesin/Shutterstock Images, 32–33; C. Winegarden/iStockphoto, 34–35, 45; George Grall/National Geographic Image Collection/Getty Images, 38; Jad Davenport/National Geographic Image Collection/Getty Images, 40

Editor: Marie Pearson
Series Designer: Joshua Olson

Library of Congress Control Number: 2020948179

Publisher's Cataloging-in-Publication Data

Names: Huddleston, Emma, author.
Title: Animal encounter bucket list / by Emma Huddleston
Description: Minneapolis, Minnesota : Abdo Publishing, 2022 | Series: Travel bucket lists | Includes online resources and index
Identifiers: ISBN 9781532195228 (lib. bdg.) | ISBN 9781644947302 (pbk.) | ISBN 9781098215538 (ebook)
Subjects: LCSH: Travel--Juvenile literature. | Animal sanctuaries--Juvenile literature. | National parks and reserves--Juvenile literature. | Wildlife viewing sites--Juvenile literature. | Zoos--Juvenile | Vacations--Juvenile literature.
Classification: DDC 910.20--dc23

CONTENTS

A TRIP TO SEE ANIMALS

Erin's hair flew behind her in the warm wind. Through her sunglasses, she looked out at the grassy plains of Lake Manyara National Park in Tanzania. She was on a safari. A local man was driving her family through the park. The truck she rode in had open windows. She enjoyed being in the open air. She saw herds of zebras. Giraffes' heads poked out of treetops in the distance. She snapped some pictures with her camera.

Giraffes are one of many species that thrive in Lake Manyara National Park.

RESORTS

Disney's Animal Kingdom Resort in Florida is a lodge where people can view wildlife up close. The hotel is located on 43 acres (17 ha) of land where more than 30 species of wild African animals live. Zebras, giraffes, flamingos, and more may walk past a hotel window at any time. Disney's Animal Kingdom Park is close to the resort. People can go on a safari there. They can see lions, gorillas, and elephants.

Erin's family had been in Tanzania for two weeks. As she and her family made their way past the zebras and giraffes, Erin remembered some of the sites they had visited earlier in their trip. At the Ngorongoro Crater, they had spotted lions, rhinoceroses, and gazelles. And at Serengeti National Park, they had been lucky enough to see a wildebeest migration.

Now a bump on the dirt track shifted Erin in her seat and brought her attention back to the present. The truck was headed toward a patch of trees. It stopped while still far from the trees, and suddenly Erin heard

Visitors can sometimes spot large herds of wildebeests at Ngorongoro Crater.

an elephant. She got her camera ready. A herd of elephants slowly became visible as they moved out from the cluster of trees. Some elephants flapped their ears. Others waved their trunks. Erin took a few pictures and then lowered her camera to watch the majestic animals splash in a nearby pond.

A safari can be a great way to view animals in their natural habitats.

ANIMAL ENCOUNTERS

Safaris are one of many types of animal encounters. People travel around the world to hopefully catch a glimpse of wildlife. Some experiences are designed to bring people to animals in natural habitats. Others, such as zoos, bring animals to people.

Most importantly, tourists need to be careful that their trips do not harm animals. Research is the first step for a responsible animal encounter. When planning a trip to see animals, look for signs that the animals are respected. If captive, the animals need proper shelters. Clean water should be available. Animals should have space to roam away from people. Tourists should stay away from places that don't take good

PERSPECTIVES

ORANGUTAN MISSES ZOO VISITORS

In 2020, a global virus pandemic was raging. The disease was COVID-19, which causes respiratory problems. Many businesses, including zoos, temporarily closed. People stayed home to try to slow the spread of the virus. Like other zoos, the Toronto Zoo closed to the public. Andrew Lentini, the director of wildlife and science at the zoo, realized some animals missed seeing people. Lentini said, "One of our oldest residents here is an orangutan named Puppe who just loves to watch people and particularly loves children. . . . not having guests here, she misses that a little bit."

Many small animals, such as chipmunks, can be common around a neighborhood.

care of their animals. They should look for places that work to meet the animals' mental needs in addition to physical needs. For example, hiding food throughout an enclosure allows animals to use their noses and brains to figure out where their meal is.

People can see and experience wildlife in many ways. They can watch animals in their neighborhoods, or they can travel to another country. Some sites are dedicated to protecting animals as well as their natural habitats. Of course, wild animal encounters are the most natural.

STRAIGHT TO THE
SOURCE

Journalist Natasha Daly saw that some animals that were part of tourist attractions were mistreated. Daly wrote:

> *Wildlife tourism isn't new, but social media is setting the industry ablaze, turning encounters with exotic animals into photo-driven bucket-list toppers. Activities . . . are shared instantly with multitudes of people by selfie-taking backpackers, tour-bus travelers, and social media "influencers" through a tap on their phone screens. . . .*

> *For all the visibility social media provides, it doesn't show what happens beyond the view of the camera lens. People who feel joy and exhilaration from getting close to wild animals usually are unaware that many of the animals at such attractions live [in horrible conditions].*

Source: Natasha Daly. "Suffering Unseen." *National Geographic*, June 2019, nationalgeographic.com. Accessed 7 May 2020.

CONSIDER YOUR AUDIENCE

Review this passage closely. Consider how you would adapt it for a different audience, such as your younger friends. What is the most effective way to get your point across to this audience? How does your new approach differ from the original text, and why?

SITES THAT CARE FOR ANIMALS

One type of place where people can see wild animals is a rehabilitation sanctuary. Rehabilitation sanctuaries protect animals. They take in injured or ill animals. They rescue animals from irresponsible owners. They give specialized care if needed. Sanctuaries try to return animals to the wild when possible. But animals may stay at a sanctuary for life. They can't go back into the wild if they grew up in captivity. A wolf may not know how to hunt. A panther may

Some sanctuaries specialize in certain species of animals, such as wolves.

have had its claws or teeth removed, so it can't hunt or protect itself. In these cases, the sanctuary tries to help the animal live in as natural a way as possible while still being cared for.

Zoos are also popular places to see animals. Zoos are different from sanctuaries because zoos focus less on rescue and recovery. Zoos show animals to the public. Some are research centers. They help animals in many ways. Animals have clean living spaces and enough food and water. They get regular veterinary care. Seeing wild animals helps educate the public. People learn about different species and their habitats. Visitors learn what threatens the animals in the wild and how people can help. Zoos study animals and help keep endangered species from going extinct. Researchers at zoos find ways to help animals survive and increase their populations.

SANCTUARIES

At Boon Lott's Elephant Sanctuary (BLES), a huge elephant uses its trunk to splash water onto its back. People watch from a distance and smile. BLES is in Thailand. The sanctuary cares for elephants. Its location in Thailand is important because many elephants there are harmed by tourism businesses.

BLES takes several steps to protect the elephants. It purposefully has low numbers of visitors at a time.

Elephants have room to roam and find food at BLES.

The workers remind people to be respectful and not get too close. Sometimes visitors help with cleanup and repair tasks around the park. BLES aims to restore its elephants' health and care for their needs.

Another sanctuary that attracts tourists is the Sloth Sanctuary of Costa Rica. Visitors begin by learning about sloths. They stand by enclosures where they can watch sloths nap and climb. They learn about sloths' habitat, diet, and behavior. Then visitors float down the Estrella River for more than an hour. An experienced boatman guides the tour. Visitors have the chance to see wild sloths hanging from tree limbs. They may see other animals in the rain forest too.

SAN DIEGO ZOO

The San Diego Zoo in California is one of the largest zoos in the United States. It's home to more than 3,500 animals from 650 different species. Scientists from the zoo work around the world. Teams on six of the seven continents do research projects to save animals. The San Diego Zoo helped save the California condor from extinction. In the 1980s and 1990s as few as 25 of these birds were left in the wild. So the zoo made a special enclosure for the condors. It carefully bred the birds to keep the offspring as healthy as possible. Eventually numbers rose. Several birds were released back into the wild. In 2017 there were 290 California condors living in the wild.

Visitors to the San Diego Zoo can watch zookeepers care for some of the animals.

Today, visitors at the San Diego Zoo can join in a variety of experiences. They can climb aboard a purple double-decker bus for a tour of the whole zoo. They can walk through gardens and see orchids, ferns, and more. At animal shows and animal encounter stations,

WORLD-FAMOUS
ZOOS

There are many famous zoos throughout the world. But they are all famous for different reasons. Which one do you think is the most impressive and why?

OLDEST ZOO
Vienna Zoo in Austria, opened 1752

LARGEST LAND AREA
North Carolina Zoo, 2,600 acres (1,100 ha)

MOST SPECIES
Zoo Berlin in Germany, 1,200 species

LARGEST AQUARIUM
Chimelong Ocean Kingdom in China, 12.87 million gallons (48.72 million L) of water

PERSPECTIVES

SANCTUARY AT THE ZOO

Bristol Zoo in the United Kingdom is one of the oldest zoos in Europe. It opened in 1836. The zoo opened an amphibian section in the 2010s. Here, staff breed two frog species at risk of going extinct. The sanctuary researches the frogs as well as other amphibians. It aims to understand threats, such as diseases, that harm many amphibians. It educates zoo visitors about amphibians. In 2010, Neil Maddison of the Bristol Zoo explained the importance of saving animal species. He said, "Biodiversity, the variety of life on Earth, is essential to sustaining the living networks and systems that provide us all with health, wealth, food, fuel and the vital services our lives depend on."

zookeepers give people a detailed look at some animals. Zookeepers teach people about polar bears, lemurs, camels, and giraffes.

Sanctuaries and zoos both provide valuable help to animals. They help injured or endangered animals. They research ways to protect animals in the wild. People can visit both types of places to see many animals and learn about them.

STRAIGHT TO THE
SOURCE

Ben Callison was the director of Cleveland Amory Black Beauty Ranch in Texas. The sanctuary was one of the largest in the United States. But Callison wished he didn't have a job. He said:

> *In an ideal world, my job would not exist. . . . I long for the day when animal sanctuaries are no longer needed. . . .*
>
> *We continue to get the calls every day: A family needs to find a home for their "pet" monkey that has become aggressive; . . . chimpanzees from laboratories need placement; . . . horses and donkeys are destined for slaughter; tigers living in a roadside zoo's deplorable conditions need immediate rescue and shelter. These stories are a mere glimpse of what is asked of just one sanctuary in a given week.*

> Source: Ben Callison. "Why We Need Animal Sanctuaries." *LiveScience*, 7 Nov. 2014, livescience.com. Accessed 7 May 2020.

BACK IT UP

The author of this passage is using evidence to support a point. Write a paragraph describing the point the author is making. Then write down two or three pieces of evidence the author uses to make the point.

NATIONAL PARKS

Countries around the world have national parks. One difference between a sanctuary and national park is that the animals in national parks are truly living in the wild. They can come and go as they please. National parks protect all wildlife, not just animals. They try to keep plants and whole habitats safe and healthy.

Some national parks are known for a particular species that lives there. Volcanoes National Park in Rwanda has five volcanoes

People can hike to see mountain gorillas in Volcanoes National Park.

in it. They are covered in lush green vegetation. This is the smallest but most-visited park in Rwanda. The government made the land a park to protect wildlife. The site is especially famous for its treks, or hikes, to see mountain gorillas. Mountain gorillas are endangered. There are only approximately 1,000 left in the wild. This park is one of the few places people can see mountain gorillas in the wild.

UNDER THE SEA

Not all animal encounters happen on land. One of the largest marine parks in the world is the Natural Park of the Coral Sea. It's located on the coast of New Caledonia in the Pacific Ocean. It protects 500,000 square miles (1.3 million square km) of ocean. That area is twice the size of France. Five sea turtle species and 48 shark species are among the animals that call it home. It has one of the biggest coral reef systems in the world.

The park is kept natural. Citizens of New Caledonia and scientists are the main visitors, though tourism companies also arrange trips in the park. Scientists snorkel in the coral reefs. They swim among brightly colored fish, sharks, and other marine life. They study how to save endangered species and how to keep the habitat healthy.

COOL PARKS

Some people enjoy seeing animals in cold climates. Greenland's Northeast Greenland National Park is the world's northernmost park. It covers 375,000 square miles (970,000 sq km). Most people must get permission from the Ministry of Nature and Environment to travel to and stay in the park. Visitors have the chance to see Arctic species such as the

NAMIB-NAUKLUFT

Namib-Naukluft National Park in Namibia is located in the world's oldest desert, the Namib Desert. The park opened in 1979. It has sand dunes and provides a dry habitat for wildlife. Species that live there can survive with little water. People who visit may encounter animals such as snakes, geckos, and hyenas.

musk ox. Musk oxen have two layers of thick, shaggy brown hair to keep warm in the cold. Other animals that thrive in this cold place are Arctic foxes, Arctic hares, seals, giant walruses, and polar bears.

Another cold habitat for animal encounters is Wrangell–Saint Elias National Park and Preserve. It's located in Alaska. People who travel there can see humpback whales, orcas, sea lions, and porpoises swimming in the sea. On land, they may spot brown bears and caribou. People can see Dall's sheep and mountain goats on the mountainsides. Moose can be found near lakes. Trumpeter swans nest in wetland areas in the park. As visitors drive through the park, they may catch a glimpse of a fox or porcupine crossing the road.

THE EVERGLADES

Some people prefer warm climates for animal encounters. Everglades National Park in Florida is home to the rare American crocodile. These crocodiles are

Musk oxen are related to mountain goats.

approximately 11.5 feet (3.5 m) long. The park is also an important protection site for manatees, which are a threatened species.

During the dry season, people often hike, camp, or go on guided tours. At any time, they can go bird-watching. Approximately 360 species of birds live in the park. People can kayak or go boating through muddy waters and tall grass.

People can spot many kinds of birds in the Everglades' wetlands.

PERSPECTIVES

GRIZZLY BEARS AT YELLOWSTONE NATIONAL PARK

Yellowstone National Park is located in parts of Wyoming, Montana, and Idaho. Large mammals such as grizzly bears, wolves, and bison live there. In the winter, people go to Lamar Valley to see many of these mammals.

Doug Peacock started an organization that protects the grizzly bears in Yellowstone. He says, "Living out on the land with the grizzly bear, you're not the dominant creature, and you're physically aware of that. . . . To make a friend of that kind of fear—it really does expand a tolerance towards all other kinds of beings."

WORLD'S LARGEST
NATIONAL PARKS

This graph shows some of the world's largest national parks. If you could travel to one of the parks, which would you want to go to? Why? What animals do you think you would see there?

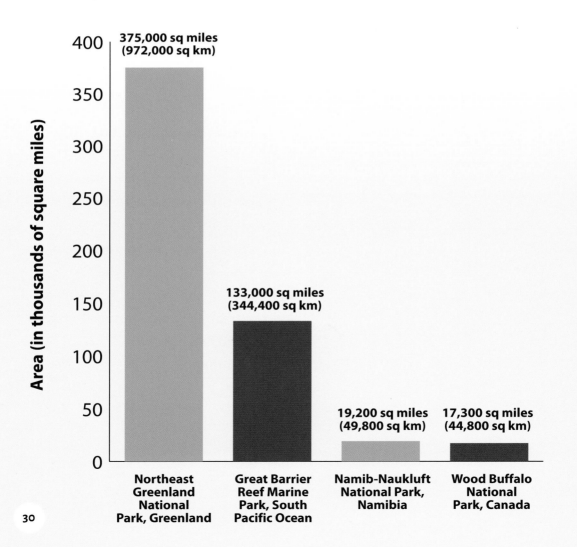

Area (in thousands of square miles)

- **375,000 sq miles (972,000 sq km)** — Northeast Greenland National Park, Greenland
- **133,000 sq miles (344,400 sq km)** — Great Barrier Reef Marine Park, South Pacific Ocean
- **19,200 sq miles (49,800 sq km)** — Namib-Naukluft National Park, Namibia
- **17,300 sq miles (44,800 sq km)** — Wood Buffalo National Park, Canada

Some tour companies offer airboat tours through the park. Airboats sit high on the water. A massive fan on the back pushes the boats along. Boaters can spot herons, turtles, raccoons, and more. People can volunteer at the park. They may get up close natural experiences while helping restore habitat and maintain the park.

National parks offer many opportunities for animal encounters. Whether a park is nearby or across the world, people can see different habitats and learn about the animals that live there.

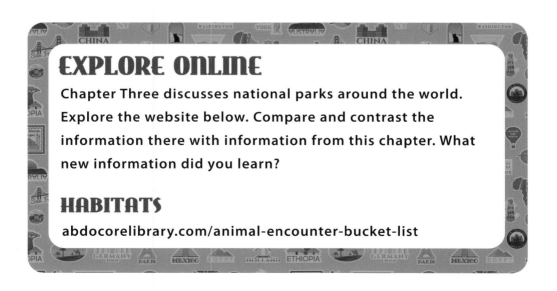

EXPLORE ONLINE

Chapter Three discusses national parks around the world. Explore the website below. Compare and contrast the information there with information from this chapter. What new information did you learn?

HABITATS

abdocorelibrary.com/animal-encounter-bucket-list

OTHER ADVENTURES

formal animal encounters such as planned trips or guided safaris can be exciting. But they aren't the only ways to get close to animals. Other adventures such as camping, hiking, spending time on the water, and bird-watching are possible to do on your own. There's no guarantee you will see a specific species. But the experience will be natural. It's important to take steps to stay safe and protect the environment on these trips.

Bird-watching can be done walking around in a person's neighborhood or at a nearby park.

Kayakers can get an up close view of a variety of wildlife.

One of the best parts of experiences such as camping, hiking, or kayaking is that people can enjoy them locally or in other countries. They can easily share the adventure with family and friends. People returning to a favorite spot can have a different wild animal encounter every time. Switching up locations gives even more opportunity to see something new.

CAMPING, HIKING, AND BIRD-WATCHING

Camping and hiking can happen anywhere. Camping in a backyard or local park lets people see insects, small mammals, and other wildlife that live nearby. Hiking gets people on the move. People can hike at a local park or nature center. They may walk through woods or up hills. They could cause wildlife to fly or scurry away at the sound of footsteps. People may see animals eating or doing other normal activities.

Even though people can camp anywhere, some sites make the experience memorable. In France at La Cabane en l'Air, or Cabin in the Air, cabins are built up to 22 feet (6.7 m) high. People are surrounded by trees and fresh air.

They see insects, squirrels, tawny owls, and other small animals.

People can bird-watch in their neighborhood. Binoculars and a field guide can make the experience even more enjoyable. But some places are especially great for seeing a lot of beautiful birds. Costa Rica is home to lots of animal species. More than 850 bird species live there, including hummingbirds and toucans. The country has tropical forests, highlands, and lowlands. Its many habitats make it a great place for wildlife to live and a great place for people to encounter animals. People from around the world go there for bird tours and more.

La Selva Biological Station in Sarapiquí, Costa Rica, offers a unique experience. It has bird-watching tours as well as a research center for students and scientists. People can walk through the rain forest on hanging bridges. Walking suspended in the air is like having a bird's-eye view.

Some people bring special equipment to spot birds and take amazing photos at La Selva Biological Station.

WATER ADVENTURES

Canoeing and kayaking are ways to encounter animals in the water. Some people kayak in rivers near their homes. They see fish swimming beneath them. Or they see birds flying above them. People can travel farther from home to kayak. Canada has many freshwater lakes. Newfoundland, Canada, is a popular place for kayaking.

People can kayak for a few hours. Or people take longer trips that last several days. Some people kayak in the ocean near the coast. On their journey, they may see whales, seals, or other sea animals. They may see puffins.

Snorkeling in the Belize Barrier Reef is an amazing animal encounter. That reef is the second-largest coral reef system in the world. It is a protected area for endangered animals such as sea turtles. There are multiple spots on the reef where people can snorkel. Two popular sites include the South

VOLUNTEERING WITH ANIMALS

People can volunteer at local humane societies and spend time with animals such as dogs and cats. Not only do they get to encounter animals, they can help out. Volunteers often walk dogs, play with cats, brush horses, clean stalls, and do other tasks. Humane societies are organizations that aim to rescue animals. Puppies, horses, and other animals may have been neglected or abused. Humane societies take animals out of those bad situations. They give them medical care and often find them new homes.

Some people dive in the Belize Barrier Reef. They can spot animals such as lobsters.

Water Caye Marine Reserve and Lighthouse Reef Atoll.

People can see many fish and corals there. Rarer animals

include manatees and whale sharks.

Whether traveling the world or sticking close to home, animal encounters are exciting ways to learn about and appreciate nature. People can go on a variety of adventures, including safaris, treks, camping, and bird-watching. Going to sanctuaries and national parks lets people see wildlife in protected places. Visiting zoos gives people a chance to learn about and see animals up close. Some animal encounters are planned. Others happen when people least expect it.

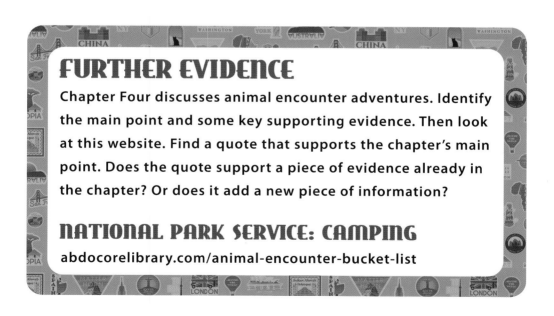

FURTHER EVIDENCE

Chapter Four discusses animal encounter adventures. Identify the main point and some key supporting evidence. Then look at this website. Find a quote that supports the chapter's main point. Does the quote support a piece of evidence already in the chapter? Or does it add a new piece of information?

NATIONAL PARK SERVICE: CAMPING

abdocorelibrary.com/animal-encounter-bucket-list

MAP

Pacific Ocean

Atlantic Ocean

1. Wrangell–Saint Elias National Park and Preserve (Alaska)

2. San Diego Zoo (California)

3. Everglades National Park (Florida)

4. La Selva Biological Station (Costa Rica)

5. Belize Barrier Reef

6. Northeast Greenland National Park

7. Cabin in the Air (France)

8. Volcanoes National Park (Rwanda)

9. Lake Manyara National Park (Tanzania)

10. Ngorongoro Crater (Tanzania)

11. Boon Lott's Elephant Sanctuary (Thailand)

12. Natural Park of the Coral Sea (New Caledonia)

Arctic Ocean

Indian Ocean

Southern Ocean

STOP AND THINK

Tell the Tale

Chapter One of this book describes someone going on a safari. Imagine you are on a similar trip in East Africa. Write 200 words about the animals you encounter. How is being in the wild different from reading about it?

Surprise Me

Chapter Two discusses how some places care for animals. After reading this book, what two or three facts about animals did you find most surprising? Write a few sentences about each fact. Why did you find each fact surprising?

Say What?

Reading about animal encounters can mean learning a lot of new vocabulary. Find five words in this book you've never heard before. Use a dictionary to find out what they mean. Then write the meanings in your own words and use each word in a new sentence.

Why Do I Care?

Maybe you have not had any of the encounters described in this book. But that doesn't mean you can't think about why animal encounters matter. What can people learn from seeing or being with animals? How do sites such as sanctuaries and national parks benefit people? How have the animals that you have encountered changed the way you think about animals?

GLOSSARY

captive
kept by humans

endangered
at risk of going extinct

extinct
the state of a species having died off with no living individuals remaining

habitat
a place that provides food, water, and shelter for living things

influencer
a person who has many followers on social media

migration
movement from one location to another at a certain time of the year

safari
a tour to see wild animals

species
a specific type of living thing whose members look similar and can mate together

sustain
to support something or someone over time

threatened
at risk of becoming endangered due to low population numbers

ONLINE
RESOURCES

To learn more about animal encounters, visit our free resource websites below.

Core Library
CONNECTION
FREE! COMMON CORE MULTIMEDIA RESOURCES

Visit **abdocorelibrary.com** or scan this QR code for free Common Core resources for teachers and students, including vetted activities, multimedia, and booklinks, for deeper subject comprehension.

Booklinks
NONFICTION NETWORK
FREE! ONLINE NONFICTION RESOURCES

Visit **abdobooklinks.com** or scan this QR code for free additional online weblinks for further learning. These links are routinely monitored and updated to provide the most current information available.

LEARN
MORE

Higgins, Melissa. *Grassland Ecosystems*. Abdo Publishing, 2016.

Lanser, Amanda. *California Condor*. Abdo Publishing, 2017.

Spalding, Maddie. *Everglades National Park*. Abdo Publishing, 2017.

INDEX

About the Author

Emma Huddleston lives in the Twin Cities with her husband. She enjoys writing, reading, and swing dancing. She has visited Sarapiquí, Costa Rica, for bird-watching, and she hopes to have more cool animal experiences!